THE EVOLUTION OF A SON

DAVID L. BAXTER, JR.

The Evolution of a Son

Copyright © 2020 David L. Baxter, Jr.

All rights reserved. This book or any portion thereof may not be reproduced or used in any manner whatsoever without the express written permission of the publisher except for the use of brief quotations in a book review.

ISBN: 978-1-7343100-7-8

Printed in the United States of America.

First printing, 2020.

Book Dedication

This book is dedicated to the man and woman that God chose to give me life, My father, David L. Baxter, Sr. and my beloved mother, who is now resting in Paradise, the late, Bonnie J. Baxter. My life would not be what it is without them both.

To my wife, my #1 pusher and supporter, Kenyetta Baxter. My Lady. My Virtuous Woman (Prov. 31). Without your encouragement, love, and prayers, I couldn't have done this.

To my three children, Shekinah', Kyle, and Kyah'. It has been the utmost privilege and honor to have been chosen by God to be your father. I am responsible for training you up in the way that you should go. My prayer is for you not to depart from it, but rather build on it and continue to live for Jesus, the Christ.

To the spiritual leaders who were a part of my evolution as a son: The Late Elder Patrick Frazier, Sr., Apostle Robert Allen Vandross, and Chief Apostle Allen Hezekiah Simmons. I want to thank each of you for your impartation and example in my life. I shall never forget you as long as I live. You've made me A TRUE SERVANT AND SON.

Table of Contents

Acknowledgments vi

Forward viii

Chapter 1: The Necessity Of Evolution 1

Chapter 2: Defining Sonship 8

Chapter 3: Qualities Of A Son 16

Chapter 4: Biblical Displays Of Sonship 29

Chapter 5: Father & Son Connectivity 48

Chapter 6: Tough Love 56

About The Author 68

ACKNOWLEDGMENTS

I am so grateful for so many people that have had a hand in my becoming. There are just too many to name. However, there are a few that I would like to acknowledge as it pertains to this particular book.

I want first to give Jesus praise! When I was 14 years old, I asked him to save my soul. He forgave me of my sins, according to Roman 10:9-10. He came into my heart and made me a brand new creature (2 Corinth. 5:17). Today, I'm saved! I have a relationship with Him, and His Spirit abides in me, it's the Holy Ghost (Acts 2:2-4).

I want to thank Dr. Susan F. Wilson, whom the Lord used to win me to Christ. She has been an encourager in my spiritual walk with the Lord. She later became my Bible College Professor at the Glory to Glory College of Theology, Columbia, SC.

I want to thank the (the late) Mother Cora L. Frazier, Lady Kathy Vandross, Elect Lady, Judge Janice Y.

Simmons, Pastor Essie L. Smalls, (the late) Mother Elvenia Boyd, Rev. Sis. Mary P. Reed, Apostle Linda Stone-Travett, and the best Asst. Pastor that a Senior Pastor could ask for, Pastor Barbara Bellamy.

To my Aunt, Sherri, Uncle John and my cousin, John Moorer II, thank you for everything!

To my brother and sister, Darien and Kendra, I love you both. Thank you for supporting me.

To my good friends Quincy, Aaron, Andre' and Cardell. Thank you for being who you are in my life. I appreciate your genuine friendship and brotherhood down through the years and even now.

To my Mother in law and Father in law, thank you for your push and prayers.

I would like to end these acknowledgments, by thanking God for my spiritual daughter, Pastor Shannon L. McRae. I don't even know where to begin with telling you, thank you. You mean so much to my family and me. I want to appreciate you, especially for never giving up on me in ministry. You have always been a pusher of my potential, and I thank you. This book would not be without you! Thank you for being TRUE!

FORWARD

The Evolution of a Son is very informative, yet tremendously inspirational, and tailored for easy reading with exceptional commentary. Bishop David Baxter's writing is advanced enough to be embraced in a seminary setting, yet practical enough to be understood by young ministers everywhere. The Evolution of a Son promises to be one of the most exceptional writings by anyone. This book is a compelling read because it was birthed out of true sonship. I have known Bishop David Baxter since he was a young man. I have served as His Pastor, Presiding Elder, Overseer, Presiding Prelate, and now Chief Apostle. He has served in the church being a young man, consistent, faithful, great character, energetic, and an example to the youth. I found him to be humble, kind, generous, trustworthy, loving, gracious, and strong. He has observed my character, mannerisms, preaching, teaching, Pastoralship, and love for people. As a son, he has patterned his ministry, walk with God and Kingdom sonship after this manner. Being now a Bishop himself in the Lord's Church, he has become a powerful preacher, evangelist, pastor, Bishop, and father himself, setting the example for future sons to follow. It goes without question that this book will surely be a valuable resource for you to have in your library and a positive seed to sow in someone's life. It is not just a thought-provoking read, but a truly authentic, holy, and heartfelt book, written out of the wellsprings of his soul. After you have read this incredible book, you will be richer, wiser, and more motivated to become kingdom sons, you were created to be. Be blessed as you read.

Apostle Allen H Simmons, DD
Presiding Prelate and Chief Apostle
Sounds of Praise Pentecostal Fellowship Ministries, Inc.

CHAPTER 1

THE NECESSITY OF EVOLUTION

Let's begin by taking a look at evolution to gain clarity of its necessity relating to sonship. There are several definitions, but let's focus in on these found in Merriam-Webster Dictionary:

1. The process by which new species or populations of living things develop from preexisting forms through successive generations.

2. The historical development of a biological group (such as a race or a species).

3. A process of continuous change from a lower, simpler, or worse to a higher, more complex, or better state: GROWTH, UNFOLDING

4. The process of working out or developing.

As we look at each one of these definitions concerning evolution, some keywords stick out. Terms such as develop or development, process, change, growth, and work.

All of these things are necessary to become anything in life, period. Nobody can get anywhere worth anything and be able to stay there and function properly without going through some kind of process that develops you and gives you the tools you need to succeed at your maximum potential.

The word necessity suggests that there is a requirement or need for something. When something is a necessity, one cannot live without it. It is unavoidable, indispensable, inevitable. You have to have it to survive.

Development and processing are necessary if you want to live and last. Every company has days of training annually. The purpose of those days of training is to maintain a certain level of competency among the staff. It is also for new staff members to be oriented appropriately to work that they may be doing for the first time. The company's survival and success is depending on this.

If development and processing are needed for business success, it holds true for our homes and churches. The Bible says, Train up a child in the way he should go: and when he is old, he will not depart from it (Proverbs 22:6 KJV). The New Living Translation of this text says, "*Direct your children onto the right path, and when they are older, they will not leave it"*. Training requires someone to give direction to another. To someone who doesn't know the way yet; therefore, they need guidance by the one that does. Don't try to figure out what requires instructions, and you will miss something fundamental every time. Say what you want, but YOU NEED THE TEACHER! One thing that I've learned in my life is that every teacher is not a father, but every father has to be a teacher.

1 Corinthians 4:15 New Living Translation (NLT)

"For even if you had ten thousand others to teach you about Christ, you have only one spiritual father. For I became your father in Christ Jesus when I preached the Good News to you."

The Good News that the Apostles preached provoked change and demanded Christians to grow up. You can not RECEIVE good teaching and remain the same. The Greek word translated as "receive" in this particular teaching is *lambano*. It simply means to take, to grasp, to seize, to receive as well as to take to oneself something or someone. It means to accept it. The opposite of receiving something is to reject it, not to take it or not to accept it. Some things shift for the better in your spirit when you RECEIVE good sound teaching in your life. If you reject it, you remain the same. There is transformational power in your reception of TRUTH.

Romans 12:1-2 King James Version (KJV)

"I beseech you therefore, brethren, by the mercies of God, that ye present your bodies a living sacrifice, holy, acceptable unto God, which is your reasonable service. And be not conformed to this world: but be ye transformed by the renewing of your mind, that ye may prove what is that good, and acceptable, and perfect, will of God."

2 Corinthians 5:17 King James Version (KJV)

"Therefore if any man be in Christ, he is a new creature: old things are passed away; behold, all things are become new."

1 Peter 2:1-3 New Living Translation (NLT)

"So get rid of all evil behavior. Be done with all deceit, hypocrisy, jealousy, and all unkind speech. Like newborn babies, you must crave pure spiritual milk so that you will grow into a full experience of salvation."

Cry out for this nourishment, now that you have had a taste of the Lord's kindness. It must become the Cry of every Christian, "Make me BETTER, Lord!" Transform me. Grow me up and mature me. Help me to EVOLVE into that competent child of God that you saw from the very foundation of the world.

Jeremiah 1:4-5 King James Version (KJV)

"Then the word of the Lord came unto me, saying, Before I formed thee in the belly I knew thee; and before thou camest forth out of the womb I sanctified thee, and I ordained thee a prophet unto the nations."

I JUST WANT TO BE WHAT HE SAW!

May I say to you that one of the worst things that could ever happen to earth, to humanity, to cultures, to businesses, to families, to ministries is for it to stop evolving. What would happen if we would stop progressing? If teachers stopped teaching, and students stopped going to school? What would happen if contractors stopped learning how to build durable buildings and homes? What would happen if the doctors we currently have retired and shut down their offices, because there was no one they trusted to take their place? What if our current technological systems stopped looking for ways to get information around this world. What if we just stopped right here in life and went no further and pursued nothing else?

The Author, Alan Weisman, posed the scenario "The World Without Us." The premise was that all of a sudden, people disappear entirely from the world. "What happens next?" The rest of the book described the slow decay of buildings, roads, bridges, and other infrastructure, and the gradual encroachment of wildlife on formerly human-dominated landscapes.

Without evolution, things decline, decay, and eventually disappear. If our families (biological/spiritual) are going to live, we need males that we can train and develop into "sons." We love our daughters. We need them too, they play a very vital part in our families also, but the SEED IS IN THE SON. In Exodus 1:12-17, when Pharaoh wanted to stop Israel from progressing, he went after the male babies, the SONS. He wanted those that had the potential of being undergirded and taught to war by the present men of Israel. They would be stronger and would be wiser, an even more significant threat to the Egyptian Kingdom than their fathers.

Exodus 1:12-17 King James Version (KJV)

But the more they afflicted them, the more they multiplied and grew. And they were grieved because of the children of Israel. And the Egyptians made the children of Israel to serve with rigour: And they made their lives bitter with hard bondage, in morter, and in brick, and in all manner of service in the field: all their service, wherein they made them serve, was with rigour. And the king of Egypt spake to the Hebrew midwives, of which the name of the one was Shiphrah, and the name of the other Puah: And he said, When ye do the office of a midwife to the Hebrew women, and see them upon the stools; if it be a son, then ye shall kill him: but if it be a daughter, then she shall live. But the midwives feared God, and did not as the king of Egypt commanded them, but saved the men children alive.

Your male child possesses within him the future of your family. You must take the time to cultivate him into your SON.

Chapter 2

DEFINING SONSHIP

When we define sonship, we understand it to be a close relationship between a father and his sons. The son, under the tutelage of his father (leader), allows the father (leader) to mold and shape him into God's intended design. I say again that there is a close relationship between these two individuals. Everybody won't be able to handle this process. Let us consider the word relationship. This word brings a distinction between persons. This word cuts one from the cloth. When we have relationship, we have developed a bond that we don't have with just anyone. It's a closer connection. Being in relationship is a walk that we take together. It is a mutual agreement between two persons to walk together, heading in the same direction in life. I've got your back, and you've got mine. I'm supporting you, and you're supporting me. I love you, and you love me. WITHOUT HIDDEN MOTIVES, we're concerned about each other's heart, goals, and desires. We want to see each other make it!

We, who are in relationship with Jesus Christ, are walking with Him. That old devotional song that we grew up singing, " Walk with me Lord, while I'm on this tedious journey, I need you to walk with me. Then it says, hold my hand, guide my feet.." This song is what relationship with the Father is all about. In this mutual connection, I am His child, and He has promised to be my God. For us to build a relationship that will stand the test of time, I need Him to walk with me. Be present in my life. In every step that I take, I need to know that you're with me, taking these steps alongside me. Holding my hand and guiding my footsteps and ensuring I'm headed in the right direction. Point me in the direction that will ultimately lead me to my eternal destiny. This kind of relationship demands TRUST! I must trust that He, who leads me, has my best interest at heart and has the wisdom and the knowledge to lead me to that place.

Just like we trust Jesus Christ with our lives, we must trust the Christ in our fathers in order for them to properly "father" us. I believe my father walks with Jesus Christ; therefore, I trust his wisdom and counsel concerning my life.

Proverbs 13:20 King James Version (KJV) He that walketh with wise men shall be wise: but a companion of fools shall be destroyed.

Proverbs 13:20 New Living Translation (NLT) Walk with the wise and become wise; associate with fools and get in trouble.

A son must submit himself to the wisdom and counsel of a father. To submit to a father means more than just showing up when you're called upon. It has to do with your heart's posture toward the father, in many cases, the man of God you're submitted to. Submission is a voluntary yielding of one's self to the authority or will of another. I believe it takes love to submit. I'm permitting you to do whatever you have to do to get me to my divine destiny. A person's heart has to be at this level of submission. Spiritual fathers will find out who their real sons are as they begin to look deep into the hearts of those that claim to be submitted sons. Son, what does your heart really show about you? Many have said one thing with their mouths but did something different when they discovered what it was going to require of them — the time, the work, the discipline, the rebuke, the correction, the sacrifice. Your heart has got to be in this if you're going to be a help in ministry. Ministry isn't easy, but somebody has got to do it! If you're going to do it right, your heart has got to be in the right place.

Matthew 15:8 New Living Translation (NLT)

These people honor me with their lips, but their hearts are far from me.

Who's going to carry on this work without submitted sons? Your submission will pay off. Put your time in; payday is coming after while. We want the reward without work, and that's just not how it works. Sincere sons aren't silent. They speak loud and clear through their service to their fathers.

The Heart of Sonship

When we look at the physical heart of a human being, it is found at the center of a person's body.

All life flows from the heart. Its beat pumps life throughout the whole body. As it is in the natural, so it is in the spiritual.

Proverbs 4:23 King James Version (KJV)

Keep thy heart with all diligence; for out of it are the issues of life.

Proverbs 4:23 New English Translation (NET Bible)

Guard your heart with all vigilance, for from it are the sources of life.

When the Bible speaks of someone's heart, it is speaking of the inner PERSON. The heart refers to the whole person, including the person's mind, will, and emotions.

In 1 Samuel 16, when the Prophet Samuel was sent to Jesse's house to anoint the next King of Judah, which would come from amongst his sons, Jesse lined up all of his sons in front of the Prophet with the expectation that based upon his choice and who He thought would be the best qualified, the oil would run.

The Bible says in 1 Sam. 16:6 that Samuel "looked on" Eliab and said, "*Surely the Lord's anointed is before him.*"

Samuel noticed the physical make up of Eliab. He noticed his clothes, his build, the way he wore his hair, the way he smiled, the way he carried himself on the outside and didn't bother to search any deeper to see what kind of " heart" he had. How many times do we misjudge people based upon what we see from their outer core? When it comes to God's business and making leadership choices, we must go deeper than what we see with our physical eye before making our final decisions.

Samuel's decision was not God's decision. Many times your choice is not God's choice. As prophetic as we can be, the truth of the matter is, we have to be careful of our choice. We need an ear to hear God so that we don't make wrong moves based upon our preference. Look at what the Lord says in the following verse, But the LORD said unto Samuel, Look not on his countenance, or the height of his stature; because I have refused him: for the LORD seeth not as man seeth; for man looketh on the outward appearance, but the LORD looketh on the HEART."(1 Sam. 16:7). Sons, make sure your countenance matches your character!! Make sure that what you portray before the public is how you behave behind closed doors in private. There is nothing more sickening than a son who switches who he is behind his father's back.

Matthew 15:8 King James Version (KJV)

This people draweth nigh unto me with their mouth, and honoureth me with their lips; but their heart is far from me.

I've concluded that the real test of truth in any relationship is not in what someone does or says in a person's face. Instead, it is found in what someone does or says when a person isn't present in the room. What is your heart speaking when I'm not here to "hear" you?

People look on the outside, but God looks on the heart, on the inside. God is not looking at the physical core of a person but the inner core of a person. God sees what the person is like on the inside. Let's be clear that this physical body is not who we are; it is just the house in which we live. The real person is found beneath this frame. You are spirit first, and that's what God identifies within you.

John 4:24 King James Version (KJV)

God is a Spirit: and they that worship him must worship him in spirit and truth.

Who are you at your inner core? In your spirit, is there truth, is there genuine love, care, and concern for your father? Before you can serve him right, you've got to be able to see him right. How do you see your father? Do you honor him? Respect him? Receive correction, rebuke, and instruction from him? Can you accept what he says, even if it hurts your feelings and adjust accordingly, knowing that he has your best interest at heart? These questions cause us to step back and look at our father and ourselves to determine where we are as it pertains to our relationship. You can not correctly serve someone you can not properly see. I've got to see you right to serve you right! Jesus was born into the world and was known as "Mary's baby," the " carpenter's son." Still, as He began to grow up and began to walk out His true assignment on the earth, after going to the cross, dying for our sins, being buried in Joseph's new tomb and then rising on the third day with all power in His hands, He became King of Kings and Lord of Lord's, the Everlasting Father, the Prince of Peace, the Mighty God! My point is even though He technically is still Mary's baby boy, but after all, He has gone through and encountered for us, He has earned the right to be seen as more than that!! Never minimize the process of your father, put respect and honor on who he is in your life and let no one disrespect him in any way. After all, He's your father.

Deuteronomy 6:5

And thou shalt love the LORD thy God with all thine heart, and with all thy soul, and with all thy might.

CHAPTER 3

QUALITIES OF A SON

"It was pride that changed angels into devils. It is humility that makes men as angels."

Saint Augustine

Isaiah 14:12-14 (KJV) says, *"How art thou fallen from Heaven. Oh, Lucifer, son of the morning. How art thou cut down to the ground, which didst weaken the nations! For thou hast said in thine heart, I will ascend into Heaven, I will exalt my throne above the stars of God: I will sit also upon the mount of the congregation, in the sides of the North: I will ascend above the heights of the clouds; I will be like the most High"*.

We must understand that the son is under the authority of his father. He should never want to purpose in his heart to become equal with his father, but always to look up to him. There is a difference between aspiring to be like someone and wanting actually to be someone. Serving in ministry, some Leaders have made a significant impact on my life. Great preachers, profound teachers, examples of love, however in my conquest to find me, I've not been a carbon copy of them. My prayer has not been" Lord make me them," but rather, " Lord give me certain characteristics or attributes that they possess." In the making of any masterpiece, there is only one true original.

I don't care how many children a father has no one can ever be him exactly. They may look like him, sound like him, carry themselves like him, but there is only one authentic Him! Some can't locate the person God has originated them to be, because of their desire to be somebody that they were only created to aspire to be like. How about locate you and what God wants you to be in the earth, and He will anoint that you. In this particular passage of scripture, Isaiah 14:12 -14, we see Lucifer, who serves, during this specific time, in Heaven under the divine rule of God. He is under the authority of God. He was created by God and given a particular assignment. We see him shifting his focus from being under the authority of God to wanting to be God. He wants a seat that doesn't belong to him. It's something when the assignment you've been given is not enough. The scripture says, "for thou has said in thine heart, I will ascend into heaven." This thought shows pride was within his heart, consequently resulted in his eviction out of Heaven. Proverbs 16:18 declares that *Pride goeth before destruction, and a haughty spirit before a fall.* There is a saying that people who are overconfident or too arrogant are likely to fail. Lucifer begins to plot inwardly about how he could take the place and position of the person he was created to take instructions from! Sons let me warn you now to watch the thoughts that tiptoe through our hearts from time to time. Jeremiah 17:9 (KJV) *"The heart is deceitful above all things, and desperately wicked: who can know it?"*

I don't care how much better you think you are than your father, what you can do better than your father, what decisions or choices you would make differently than your father, stay in your place and humble yourself. Don't let your heart move you from under his hand. When pride gets in your heart, it has the potential to push you out of place. Stay submitted, and don't let PRIDE creep up in your heart! Beware of that heart disease called PRIDE!

Lucifer then says, "I will exalt my throne." He begins to plan out how to get in a place that he was not created to hold. "I will exalt my throne above the stars of God," which simply means that he wanted not only to be God, but he also wanted to have the authority over the things God had authority over. The "stars" here in this text mentioned is believed to be, by John Gill's commentary, as stars God had made and set in the heavens, and preserves or the stars referred to the angels, Job 38:7 or rather the kings and princes of the earth, over whom God placed himself, having subdued them under him. These stars may be applied to ecclesiastical persons, pastors, and bishops of churches, according to Revelation 1:20 *"I will sit also upon the mount of the congregation in the size of the North and then he says, I will ascend above the heights of the clouds. I will be like the most high."* He moves from being the servant to wanting to be served!! Lucifer wanted the POWER!

Lucifer was not satisfied with just being a servant. He had to be the one being served. It is in this place that he allows pride to turn his service to God from worship to warfare. When we look at Pride, we find out that it is a high or an ordinance opinion of one's dignity, importance, merit or superiority, whether as cherished in the mind or as displayed in conduct where the craving of compliments, fearing our image or entertaining an overly critical view of ourselves. Pride can be both glaringly obvious and deceptively sneaky. Pride turns everything into being about me, myself and I. You become the focal point. It is in this passage that we see this definition come into fruition. Lucifer began to plan deceitfully to undermine God's rule and reign in Heaven. This undermining causes a revolt in Heaven which brought violence to Heaven. Lucifer and a third of the angels that he convinced to stand with him were ultimately judged and cast out, which means Lucifer lost the place that he had in Heaven. Luke 10:18 records these words, *"And he said unto them, I beheld Satan as lightning fall from heaven."* Be careful not to want so much so soon that you become the cause of your fall.

When a son comes against his father, he will always lose. You can never be more than the one who created you. So, no matter what you do, the creator is who he is, and you or no one else can take that from him. 1 Corinthians 10:12 warns us, *"so if you think you are standing firm, be careful that you don't fall."* Psalms 10:2-11 describes the oppressive result of pride and a plea from God for justice and defense for those caught in its tailspin.

Pride is at the heart of bullying and entitlement. Its deceptive tendency leaves a wake of destruction. The very nature of human conflict is rooted in elements of pride, pride only breeds quarrels, *but wisdom is found in those who take advice* (Proverbs 13:10).

One has to be mindful of the spirit of the age. Pride is running rampant in our generation. We must be cautious that while we're serving our fathers now, we may one day be one. We must be very careful not to allow the spirit of pride to affect our humility and our service to our fathers and leaders. You reap what you sow. When you see pride trying to rise in your spirit, recognize it, acknowledge it, and then quickly cast it down; get rid of it immediately. Know that no true father is trying to keep you from anywhere or anything that God has for your life. He's trying to get you there, but the right way and in the proper condition. 1 Peter

5:6 (KJV) says, "*Humble yourselves, therefore under the mighty hand of God, that he may exalt you in due time.*"

The definition of humility, according to Merriam Webster, is the freedom from pride or arrogance. The quality or state of being humble, of being meek, of being modest. It is the absence of arrogance, assumption, egotism, hardiness, and the such like. Humility comes from the Latin word *humilitas*, which means low—having a modest opinion or estimate of one's importance or rank. When I think of humility, I think of what the Apostle Paul says in Romans 12:3 (NLT) *"Because of the privilege and authority[a] God has given me, I give each of you this warning: Don't think you are better than you really are. Be honest in your evaluation of yourselves, measuring yourselves by the faith God has given us.* The Apostle Paul makes us know that no matter what, our gifts, talents, or abilities are not to glory in what he has, as if he had not received it. What we have and can do is not of ourselves, but rather from God. He's the giver; we're the receivers. He makes it all possible. The Apostle Paul further expresses his humility by saying in 1 Corinthians 15:10 (KJV), "*But by the grace of God I am what I am: and his grace which was bestowed upon me was not in vain; but I laboured more abundantly than they all: yet not I, but the grace of God which was with me.*"

It is by God's design that everything God created, someone has to put their hands on it for it to grow. As we deal with humility, the scripture says, humble yourself under the mighty hand of God, and in due season or due time, he will exalt you. These things are necessary to mold us. Oh, the thing about it is you can't make yourself. God puts you in the hands of somebody else.

In order to receive what's in the hand of the other individual, you must be willing to humble yourself. You must be willing to submit yourself, voluntarily give up you in order to receive from them. Every one of us that desires to be anything great in the Kingdom must be made. The thing about it is you can't make yourself. God puts you in the hands of somebody else. Jeremiah 18:1-6 (KJV) *"The word which came to Jeremiah from the Lord, saying, Arise, and go down to the potter's house, and there I will cause thee to hear my words. Then I went down to the potter's house, and, behold, he wrought a work on the wheels. And the vessel that he made of clay was marred in the hand of the potter: so he made it again another vessel, as seemed good to the potter to make it. Then the word of the Lord came to me, saying, O house of Israel, cannot I do with you as this potter? Saith the Lord. Behold, as the clay is in the potter's hand, so are ye in mine hand, O house of Israel"*. Every one of us are vessels that God desires to use, but the question in this hour is, can you stand to be made?

Whose hands are you in besides God's? To come fully in line with the plan of God for your life, you must submit to a process. Every plan has a process. There are no overnight wonders in the Kingdom. Every one of us has to submit to a process. Now in that process, different layers are being added to your life that are necessary for where you're headed. Then, some layers are being removed as you mature and matriculate your way through the process. If I don't back out of the process, I will ultimately become what God has in mind for my life in him. There is an old saying that the "humble child tastes the grace". Know that humility is not a weakness; it is a strength. Pride is a weakness. Pride causes people to think of themselves more highly than they should.

If you're going to reach the place that God has for you, you must stay in a position of humility. 1 Corinthians 2:9, the Apostle Paul says, "*But as it is written, eye hath not seen, nor ear heard, neither have entered into the heart of man, the things which God hath prepared for them that love him.*" I would like to suggest to you that what is keeping us from walking in 1 Corinthians 2:9 is the lack of submission to process. This is a problem that we see profoundly in the church today. We are dealing with a lot of leaders who want to lead without being led. They want to teach without being taught. **You cannot release what you have not received**. You see, in God's process, you are not your own boss in the process of becoming great in Him.

You cannot get there on your own. You must stand on the shoulders of another leader, and can I tell you that you can't stand on my shoulders if you can't submit to my authority. Hebrews 13:17 declares, "*Obey them that have the rule over you, and submit yourselves: for they watch for your souls, as they that must give an account, that they may do it with joy, and not with grief: for that is unprofitable for you."* How are you going to get mad with your leader when they're trying to watch out for you? Sometimes your leader's "NO" is for your protection. Submission is the key to greatness. Submission is voluntary obedience. I do it because I love my Leader. You see, I obey you because of your position, but I submit to you because I love you.

There is a reward that comes through your submission. The Bible declares in the 1 Peter 5:6, *"Humble yourselves therefore under the mighty hand of God, that he may exalt you in due time."* I don't submit with the motive to be exalted, but if I submit, in due season, I will be exalted. Those that are submitted need not worry, they will not miss their season of elevation. What God has for you, it is for you, and when the time is right, he will bring it to pass. This is one of the most significant areas of attack. So many want to be so much with so little. I'm not talking about numbers. I'm talking about tenure, service, knowledge, wisdom, power, consecration, character, integrity, the right spirit. You see, these things are planted in us during the process. While you're under the hands of a leader who possesses these characteristics themselves, for one cannot produce what they don't own themselves. Your service may look to be overlooked and unseen, but know that you are great right where you serve. In 1

Samuel 16, we see this little shepherd boy by the name of David, who was the son of Jesse, who was seemingly forgotten about and pushed out into the pasture to shepherd sheep. At the same time, his brothers enjoyed the company of each other in the comfort of their father's home. The scripture reveals that when God got ready to anoint the next King of Judah, He sent the Prophet Samuel right where David was serving, and God did not allow Samuel to leave that house until he had the right one. JUST SERVE!! God knows where you are, and when He gets ready to use you in a different capacity you won't have to campaign, He will pick you out Himself.

Don't be discouraged if it seems like you're in a hidden place. Know that God never forgets.

Accountability

Merriam Webster dictionary defines accountability as an *obligation*. It is the willingness to accept responsibility or to account for one's actions. It's *answerability*.

Romans 14:12 says, "*So then every one of us must give an account of himself to God.*" Paul teaches that each one of us will be held accountable for our actions. We will answer for whatever we have decided to do in this body. If we hurt someone, we should apologize and make things right. If we take something that isn't ours, we should give it back. If we say we're going to do something, our word should be our bond. If we are given instruction or given an assignment by our Leader and accept the assignment, we then become accountable for that work and its productivity. The responsibility and the answerability cannot be thrown off on another because the instructions were given to YOU. Make sure that you are ready for what you say YES to. "As we mature and grow, holding others accountable for their words and actions enables us to live with purpose and integrity," according to TDJakes.com.

All in all, what this tells us is that we must practice letting our words be our bond. We must be trustworthy. Our leaders must be able to have faith and dependability in what we say and do.

One of the reasons why we look to God is because we have found him to be a Man of His Word. Numbers 23:19 declares, "God is not a man that he should lie; neither the son of man, that he should repent: hath he said, and shall he not do it? Or hath he spoken, and shall he not make it good"? This scripture simply tells us that we can trust God. We can depend on God. We can believe God. He's reliable. He's our resource, so if he says he's going to do something, he's going to do just what he said. He is accountable. He takes responsibility for His actions. As a matter of fact, He says in Hebrews 6:13 that when He could swear by no other, He swore by Himself.

Hebrews 6:13 (NIV) *When God made his promise to Abraham, since there was no one greater for him to swear by, he swore by himself. God took an oath in his own name.*

As a son, it must mean something when your name is called. Genuine sons don't have a problem with accountability. We understand the honor of being accountable. To have someone in your life that loves you enough and cares enough about your life to want to hold you responsible for your actions is indicative of love and concern for your wellbeing. This kind of love corrects you. This kind of love rebukes you. This kind of love directs you. This kind of love shapes you and molds you into the great Leader that you will be one day. One of the things that we struggle with in this hour is answerability. No one seems to want to answer. We just want to go about life and ministry doing what we want to do and how we want to do it without being checked, and this is not a good thing. If Jesus had to check his disciples, then our Leaders are going to have to check us. It's the only way to stay on the right path. The fact of the matter is one day we will all answer to God. We will answer for what we did and didn't do. This includes how we obeyed and served those that He placed over us to Lead us.

The Five Signs of Spiritual Sons and Daughters by Mark DeJesus emphasizes, "Sometimes we can look to spiritual fathers, but we do not take responsibility to live as sons."

And he will turn the hearts of the fathers to the children, and the hearts of the children to their fathers... **Malachi 4:10**

Here are the five signs that Mark points out that will help us to identify spiritual sons and daughters.

1. You will know them by their pursuit.
2. You will know them by their heart to serve.
3. You will know as you watch how they are able to handle authority.
4. You will notice how they handle correction.
5. You will know over time.

This cannot be rushed. Relationship, credibility, and trust must be built over time. Time will tell if someone is really serious about walking as a powerful son in the Kingdom. You will observe many with great potential fade away. Time will reveal their heart. This is all part of the journey.

CHAPTER 4

BIBLICAL DISPLAYS OF SONSHIP

"Yes, you are a son of God. But a son must have a heart to serve."

— Paul Brady

The term "sonship" when we study it from the biblical standpoint, refers to both male and female. The focus is not on gender, but on the nature of the relationship. It speaks of those of us that have been grafted into or adopted into the family of God through accepting God's Son, Jesus Christ, as our Lord and personal Savior.

Romans 8:14-16 King James Version (KJV)

For as many as are led by the Spirit of God, they are the sons of God. For ye have not received the spirit of bondage again to fear; but ye have received the Spirit of adoption, whereby we cry, Abba, Father. The Spirit itself beareth witness with our spirit that we are the children of God:

This scripture points out something significant in its 14th verse, *"For as many as are led by the Spirit of God, they are the sons of God."* I believe it is essential to bring to our attention that to be true sons, we must be willing to be led by a Father.

It's a decision that has to be made when you are determining who you want to be in the Kingdom. Am I willing to submit myself to a Father to be taught, corrected, be nurtured, receive wisdom, knowledge, and understanding?

We will look at a few biblical displays of sonship. I pray to convey to you the necessity and the value of this relationship.

JESUS

Jesus, the Son of God. The only begotten of the Father, when we examine His relationship with His Father, we see someone with a desire to please his father genuinely. For example, when we see Jesus in the Garden of Gethsemane. He is there out of obedience to the Father. He is uncomfortable, yet remains committed to the cause. *"My Father, if it is possible, let this cup pass from Me; nevertheless not as I will, but as thou wilt."* (Matt.26:39b KJV) There will be assignments that the father will request of you to do, and you can't pass the buck. It's your assignment, and no matter how difficult it may be, because of your desire to please the father, you must go through with it. This assignment may cause you to deal with people you don't want to deal with, encounter problems that you have never dealt with before; it may challenge you beyond what you are used to but trust him! There is something in you that the world needs, and the only way they're going to get what it is that they need is that you be willing to be temporarily inconvenienced. Believe me, when I tell you, God has strengthened you for THIS moment. Look at Jesus's level of submission here in this garden. He's just received a glimpse of what He is about to go through, and when He talks to His Father, He gets "real "with Him. He doesn't hide how He feels; He doesn't pretend to be happy about what has just been presented to Him. I want to say to every son, you need a father that you don't have to pretend in front of when you need to talk about issues that you're going through or how you're feeling at certain points and times in your life. Even when it comes down to ministry, you need a father that you can become vulnerable with and know that he's got you at that moment, and it's ok to share your heart. I like the way the Message Bible translates what Jesus said in this verse. Here it is, *"My Father if there is any way, get me out of this."* Now I'm going to finish this, but I had to stop right there to give someone a chance to reflect upon those moments when you may have thought after seeing some things that you would have to go through in ministry where you said or even thought, " Now Lord, you sure?" "I mean... come on, God... are You serious right now?" Ha! "Lord, there's got to be another way!" "I don't want THIS, GET ME OUT OF THIS!" Isn't it something that after Jesus got finished expressing His feelings that He concludes that it's not about His will, but the Father. He says, *"But please, not what I want. You, what do you want?"* When we get finished expressing our feelings, let's come back to what it's all about, fulfilling the father's will. I love that about Jesus. Throughout scripture, as Jesus walked and did miracles, signs, and wonders, He remained focused on the fact that He was here fulfilling the will of His Father. I thought about something that has just blessed me. I received my first pastoral assignment in April 2003. I was serving faithfully as an ordained Elder at Greater New Bethel SOP under the tutelage of Bishop Allen H. Simmons. There was a dire need in Columbia, SC, at a covenant ministry that was without a pastor. I wasn't looking to be sent out because I was enjoying my current role at my home church. I found out that when you serve well, and the father needs you, he'll snatch you while you're serving and put you where He needs you at that moment; You've got to be alright with that. Adjust and keep on serving. I didn't necessarily want to go, but a son learns how to adjust to what the father needs. What an adjustment that was for my family and me. It wasn't what I wanted, but my father sent me. I pastored there for seven years. God blessed us through our many challenges that come with building and maintaining ministry. Souls were saved and added to the church. We worked with people through deliverance, salvation, and many received the baptism of the Holy Ghost. Yes, Deliverance Cathedral SOP, as the Lord had us name the church we were sent to pastor. Back then, we had Friday night evangelistic services, and it wasn't a lot of us at that time, but boy oh boy, you would've thought the church was full once we got stirred in there. During this time, about two years into Pastoring there, the Lord led me to begin a ministry back in a town that I attended church in when I was a little boy coming up in the St. George/Reevesville, SC area. So much was happening for us as it pertains to working ministry and establishing work. Later, at DCSOP, we had to make some physical moves due to facility issues. And once we got settled in this particular building, I experienced my best year there. I began to see the fruit of my labor. People were coming in off the streets, receiving Christ in their hearts. The people of God were working extremely well together. We did some major upkeep and beautifying of the sanctuary, and we were set. So many great things happened that 7th year! In October 2010, we headed to the SOPPFM International Holy Convocation with great excitement. We had an immensely explosive experience during Holy Convocation. On the final day of the meeting, it was time to receive appointments. My Spiritual Father, the Chief Apostle, announced that He was sending me to Myrtle Beach, SC, to Pastor True

Light SOP! My heart dropped. Tears welled up in my eyes, and I couldn't believe that I was being sent somewhere else. I couldn't imagine being pastor anywhere else. My wife and I are builders. To go somewhere where we didn't have to start with 2 or 3 was a major culture shock for us, but the biggest shock was to leave the ones that we worked with and nurtured and walked through major issues. Many of them lived in our home. We helped find jobs, fill out applications, find clothes to wear, helped settle them, and grow them up as adults. We were young, but they had babies, and we became grandparents because there was no one else to look at as such. What a hard pill to swallow to have to make this move. I remember our first Sunday at True Light. Pastor Bellamy and Pastor King, who was Bro. JJ at that time and some others were waiting outside to welcome us to the church. That was different! We drove up in our Orange Honda Accord (literally laughing out loud), and they received us with loving genuine smiles and showed us into what was now going to be my office. Pastor King helped me get dressed and then escorted me out to the pulpit, and they escorted my wife to her seat where she would now sit, and we cried. One of the things my father asked me that still sticks with me today "Do you trust me?" and I answered him back, "Yes sir." With tears in my eyes that Sunday, we danced, and I preached, and we made it through, but we still missed Deliverance Cathedral and Cathedral of Hope. I said all of that to say this, as a son, you're not going to like or always agree with every decision your father makes concerning you, but if you know that he genuinely loves you and has your best interest at heart, TRUST HIM! Here we are almost ten years later, and I can't begin to tell you how God has blessed us as we continue to serve faithfully and humbly at what is now The Greater True Light Ministries SOP and The Cathedral of Hope Ministries SOP.

Let's look at Jesus when He was led into the wilderness to be tested by the devil. The scriptures declare first of all in Matthew 3:16-17 New Living Translation (NLT) *"After his baptism, as Jesus came up out of the water, the heavens were opened[a] and he saw the Spirit of God descending like a dove and settling on him. And a voice from Heaven said, "This is my dearly loved Son, who brings me great joy."* There is nothing like hearing your father say, "I'm proud of you, or I am pleased with you." There is something about hearing those words that give a son more fuel to remain faithful to their assignment and their assignment giver. Fathers, if you have a good son and he's obedient, submissive, humble, and works hard to fulfill assignments and tasks given to him, tell him how PROUD you are of him. If he has brought shame to your name and but has worked hard to recover and realign, tell him that you're PROUD of him. Many times, sons are trying all they know how to be the best man that they can be and yet fall short at times of what you expect. Don't go for the mistake, the error, fault, or flaw first all the time.

Encourage and point out the good first and then advise or correct where needed in a way that they don't feel attacked or beat down. This father in this text says to his son I love you, and I'm proud of you. Hearing the words," I love you, and I'm proud of you" has the potential of giving a son the ammunition needed to face the wilderness in his life. The devil is going to try him just like he did Jesus with temptation, but because of the words that fell from your lips, before he went in, he will come out of it with the victory. You see, in the wilderness where Jesus was tempted of the devil, every time the devil came at him with temptation, Jesus had a word to combat him from His Father. He remembered what his father said before him coming in contact with this situation. Fathers, your voice is so needed in the lives of your sons. There will come a time as we live our lives that we will hear your voice telling us what to do, or we will remember a conversation that you had with us, and the answer to our now situation will be found in our Last conversation with you. In that wilderness, the father wasn't physically present with Jesus, his son, but what Jesus says and what Jesus knows and uses to fight off the adversary pays homage and great respect to what he has received from the father. The victory, if you will, was in his ability to hold fast to the word of God while going through his wilderness experience. The devil will not defeat me because I've got a word from God. How many things have you come through, because you remembered what your daddy told you? I don't know about anyone else, but I don't struggle with giving credit to whom credit is due or honor to whom honor is due. I will be the first to say who I am and where I am in my life is a result of the examples of manhood and fatherhood that I have had in my life. I thank God often for my biological father, David L. Baxter, Sr. and the Spiritual Fathers that I was blessed to come in contact with that had a hand in my upbringing. My Pastors, The Late Elder Patrick Frazier Sr., born and raised under his leadership. I was saved, sanctified, and received the gift of the Holy Ghost as a young member of his church. I remember the night the Lord saved me there. We were in revival, his daughter, Dr. Susan Wilson, was what we called " running" the revival, and I received salvation along with many other young people during that revival. Oh, what a time that was that week. I received the gift of the Holy Ghost that same week, home in my mother's bathroom. I came home from revival and went in there to pray because I wanted the Holy Ghost, and He filled me that night with the evidence of speaking in other tongues as the Spirit gave me utterance. Yes, Lord! I was called to preach sometime later under Elder Frazier's tutelage at the age of 16yrs old, and he encouraged me and let me preach and later allowed me to receive my license in the FBH as a Local Minister. At the age of 18, I was led to Apostle Robert A Vandross, who took me under his wings and taught me so much about evangelistic ministry. He would preach revival after revival, week after week. We would be all over. I was in High School when I first met him and his family, but he was so instrumental in my learning the ropes of evangelism. He and his wife took me like I was one of their children, and we still have that close relationship today. Then came, my Chief Apostle Allen H. Simmons. I had known him for many years as a young boy coming up in the FBH Church and had always been around New Bethel as my mom was once a member there. I had always admired him and his church. You're talking about a preacher and a singer and a praiser. The anointing was and is still unexplainable upon his life, and as a young boy coming up, I always wanted to sit under his tutelage and be a part of his church. Not knowing some years later, that it was in the plan of God the whole time. I've come to realize that timing is everything. When my wife and I decided that we were going to get married, I went to my pastor at that time, who was Apostle Vandross, and talked with him about it, and he released me to go to be with Apostle Simmons and New Bethel SOP. I began working there under Apostle's teaching and what a deposit and difference he has made in my life. He is one of the kindest, most humble, most genuine, most loving men I know. He has a way of making each person feel special. He is a people's person. And he became my example. I observed him carefully and served him fully. I did my best not to give him any trouble. I don't think I did, but if I did, his rebuke was laced with so much love and care that I just took it and went away thinking to myself, did I just get rebuked? He has taught me everything I know about Leadership and Pastoring. He is continuously imparting wisdom nuggets about ministry, marriage, financial stability, and family. It has been a journey, but a joy learning from him and can I say that I'm still learning. We will never know it all. He is my Spiritual Father and Leader, and I will always have respect for him and look up to him as long as I live. What I am trying to convey to you is your father's voice counts! *If you listen, you'll live!* He's been where you're going. It may be a different time, but it's the same temptations. Keep that voice in your ear.

DAVID

Other examples of good sonship would be David, one who kept his posture as a son and didn't run toward the position. He served his father, and the position came to him. His heart was pure. He didn't have to be seen or heard. He just did what he was assigned to do, and when God was ready to use him, he called for him and anointed him in his father's house, in the midst of his brethren for the task. I love David, because as a son, He wasn't in a hurry to be anybody else, but who he was. He waited until it was his turn. Just an observation from the service of David as a son, learn to be consistent at being committed. Jesse, his father, didn't have to wonder about whether the sheep and the pastures would be taken care of because David was consistent with being in place performing his duties. When Samuel asked the question to Jesse, " Is this all of your sons?" Jesse knew exactly where David was even though he didn't want him to be seen or didn't think he was the one that the Lord wanted to anoint and appoint as the next king over Judah. He had not taken the time to prepare David for this task, but God had been on the job from the beginning. God used animals to prepare David for leading people. I need to tell some son, don't take your unseen service for granted, you're being prepared behind the scenes for something that will be seen by everyone in God's own time. Stay put in the pasture, because promotion is coming! I wished more of us were like David, work without worrying about being promoted. If I'm never taken any higher than serving the sheep and keeping the pasture clean, if it's what God wants me to do, I'll do it joyously, because I know that I'm pleasing God. (I Sam.16:1-13)

THE PRODIGAL SON

The Prodigal Son gets my respect because he represents to me the repented son. The prodigal son moves out of his father's house too fast. He wasn't prepared for what he is asking for from his father. However, he was released with the inheritance that he has asked for from him. Let me put a pin here to just say as a son, you don't have to ask for your inheritance. If something is for you, it will come to you. This son gets his portion of the inheritance prematurely, and he immediately becomes wasteful and riotous with his living. The scripture records that he spends all that he has been given and has nothing to show for it. Now, a famine arises in the land, and he has nothing to survive off and ends up in lack. The purpose of the inheritance is that you will have something to build upon to make a living and continue to live. Father's prepare for the future. Sons, don't take what your father has developed and worked hard for and throw it away with handling business nonchalantly. Fathers, your sons may pitch a fit, get upset, feel you don't care about them, and think you're doing them wrong, but that's your inheritance, **hold it until they can handle it!** They will appreciate it once they've matured a bit. Your life and the things that are connected to it are your responsibility. This son spent all of the portion of his father's inheritance that was given to him, and now he is in need in a time where he should be in a place to help others that are in need. The purpose of the inheritance is for you to build upon, not to spend at your leisure. It is in the famine where the prodigal son earns my respect.

Luke 15:15-19, *"He persuaded a local farmer to hire him, and the man sent him into his fields to feed the pigs. The young man became so hungry that even the pods he was feeding the pigs looked good to him. But no one gave him anything. "When he finally came to his senses, he said to himself, 'At home, even the hired servants have food enough to spare, and here I am dying of hunger! I will go home to my father and say, "Father, I have sinned against both Heaven and you, and I am no longer worthy of being called your son. Please take me on as a hired servant."*

This part of the prodigal son's story shows the turning that begins to take place in this young man's mind. He finally comes to the place where he begins to think; things are not going to get any better in my life with me going in the direction that I am going. I have got to do something about this. The first thing he does is goes to try to find a job. He gets this job of feeding pigs. The scripture declares that he got so hungry until he was about to eat the pigs' food because no one gave him food to eat. It was at that point in his life when the Bible records that this son "comes to himself." He comes to his senses. He realizes that what he is doing and the way he's been living is beneath his privilege. He drops his pride, humbles himself, and says, I'm going back home. I'll deal with whatever consequences I'll have to deal with when I get there, but one thing I do know and that is anything is better than living like this.

I'm afraid that pride has many of our sons in a sunken place, but I want you to know that you don't have to stay in that place, you can come back home. Maybe you messed up, and perhaps you made some wrong moves and decisions. Maybe you reacted at the moment, and you walked away prematurely. Maybe you were coerced by someone else out of your place.

Drop your pride, humble yourself, and make that call, get in your car and make that drive. Whatever you must do, get on your way back home to your father. He's awaiting your return more than you know. The prodigal son earns my respect because when he comes to his senses, he doesn't stay away from his father. He returns apologetically, sincerely, and genuinely home to say, "Dad, I apologize for what I did, I wasn't ready like I thought I was, but if you'd just take me back in the house.... I don't even have to be called your son, you can make me one of your servants, and I'll be fine, because at least I know I'm back where I'm supposed to be, home with my father". We may not like what he did, but we must respect him for how he recovers. We know the rest of the story. His father sees him coming from afar, runs out to meet him, and calls a whole celebration for his return!

Luke 15:20-24 New Living Translation (NLT)

So he returned home to his father. And while he was still a long way off, his father saw him coming. Filled with love and compassion, he ran to his son, embraced him, and kissed him. His son said to him, 'Father, I have sinned against both Heaven and you, and I am no longer worthy of being called your son.[a]' "But his father said to the servants, 'Quick! Bring the finest robe in the house and put it on him. Get a ring for his finger and sandals for his feet. And kill the calf we have been fattening. We must celebrate with a feast, for this son of mine was dead and has now returned to life. He was lost, but now he is found.' So the party began.

There will be a Celebration for your Submission!

ABSALOM

When we look at Absalom, we find out that he is the third son of King David by Maacah. When we read concerning the description of him, it is said that no man in Israel was as handsome as his appearance. Everyone seemed to love Absalom. The problem begins when his half-brother, Ammon, one of David's other sons, falls in love with his sister Tamar and rapes her. For two years, Absalom keeps silent, sheltering Tamar in his home with the expectation that David would punish Ammon for this act of incest in their family. When David does nothing, Absalom, in his anger, plotted to have his half-brother Ammon killed as revenge for what he did to their sister Tamar. Fathers, we must learn how to deal with difficult situations in our homes and ministries. Many of us hesitate and procrastinate because we dislike confrontation. Many times, we do this because we don't know what to say. We do not have the answer or how about this, we don't know how to comfort our family during times of crisis. This is a severe matter, and two years later, nothing has been said or done concerning the rape of a daughter by her own brother. Situations that are left not dealt with have the potential of causing bitterness in the hearts of those affected by it. This has affected Absalom to the place that his heart has been turned against his brother and his father. He has his brother killed, runs away to a place called Geshur, where he lived with his grandfather in hiding for three years. In this midst of all this, David yet loves Absalom dearly and mourns his absence, the Bible says in 2 Sam. 13:37 "day after day." Finally, the Bible records that David allows Absalom to come back home. There it is again, a father who loves his son despite his wrongdoing welcomes him back home. The thing that differs between the prodigal son and Absalom is that Absalom, after being allowed back home, gradually begins to undermine his father, King David. Absalom began to usurp his father's authority and speak against him to the people. He used his charm to work his way into the hearts of many of the people so that they would follow him and not his father. Now, if that ain't a bad spirit! Do you even understand the danger that you put yourself in when you try to conspire against your leader, not to mention your father? Absalom lied to his father and asked for permission to go to Hebron to worship God when he was going to be made a king. He gathered an army. He sent messengers throughout the land, proclaiming that he was king. Can you imagine how David feels? His son, whom he raised, has now behind his back raised an army against him to try to take his place. Anything that is done in dishonor will not last. It will fail unless you repent. Absalom was dishonest and dishonorable, yet he had significant influence, but God was with his father, David, and so were many other people who served David down through the years. Listen, I don't care who turns on you; everybody isn't going to turn. Somebody is going to remain committed and faithful to you as their leader. Good leaders are hard to find, so when you get a good leader stick with them. We are all subject to situations such as this one, where sometimes the persons closest to us will try to undermine our authority. Keep your eyes and ears open. Don't be paranoid, just pay attention to details, because it's often hidden in the details.

When David learns of the rebellion, he and his people flee to Jerusalem. Even in Absalom's rebellion, his father orders him not to be harmed. Sometimes as sons in your rebellion, you have no idea what you're doing. When you come against your father, God will make a fool out of you. Look at what happened to Lucifer when he tried God, The Father. He was humiliated and kicked out of Heaven. He lost his place for eternity! Are you prepared for what your rebellion is going to cost you? So, it happens that David's army and Absalom's army ends up clashing at Ephraim, and the army of David was victorious! Absalom, running to escape the battle, was riding a mule under a tree, and his hair got entangled in the branches. The mule kept going, and Absalom was left hanging in the branches by his hair with no one to get him down. Joab, one of David's generals, took three javelins and thrust them into Absalom's heart. Then ten of Joab's armor-bearers circled Absalom and killed him. Be careful of the setup, because it may not work out in your favor.

Sons never undermine or conspire against your fathers, stand by their side, and support them and help them, and they will remember you. Don't try to get over, but be willing to go through. Absalom was selfish and used his good looks and personality to gain the support of people, but in the end, it wasn't enough to keep him alive. (2 Sam. 18:1-17)

Chapter 5

FATHER & SON CONNECTIVITY

Dictionary.com defines connectivity as *the state or quality of being connected or connective.* It is the ability to link to and communicate with others. It is a relationship between two people who have things in common that join them together or cause them to associate. When we have connectivity, we feel in touch with someone who cares about us. We don't feel left alone. We feel a sense of belonging. Brothers and sisters, connection is essential to human life. We were not built as humans to live in this world alone. When God made Adam, he looks at Adam walking and working in the Garden of Eden, and he says in Gen. 2:18, *"And the Lord God said, It is not good that the man should be alone; I will make him an help meet for him."* Eve would be his helper, partner, companion, lover, a helper comparable to him. She would be someone that Adam could connect with. This connection would take place through a relationship.

They connect because they can relate. When we understand a relationship and see it modeled in Genesis and throughout scripture, we find that a truly authentic relationship is founded upon trust. This trust is not received overnight, but rather through a proving process that we both undergo that shows both parties that we're safe with each other. You can trust me, and I can trust you. Trusting someone is a decision that one has to make.

> *"Most good relationships are built on mutual trust and respect"*
>
> — Mona Sutphen

I often say you can't trust everybody, but you can trust somebody. It is when you find that person you can trust that connectivity begins. You then gain that sense of being open and free to another person as they are open and free with you with respect as our standard and parameter. As this pertains to a *father and son connection*, this is often an area of much hesitation. For both the father and the son are not always as open and accessible as they should make themselves for each other. However, it is needed for the proper evolution of that son. He needs a father that is not afraid to sit down and converse with him. There needs to be conversations held about what is essential to both of them. Sometimes that son needs a listening ear without judgment after he's finished talking. As fathers, we can make it hard for our sons to come to us about things that they are dealing with because we oftentimes do not hear them out or are quick to pass judgment on them. Be intentional at listening. Hear him out before responding, because your response may change after he's finished talking. Remember, you're establishing connectivity with your son. You're all he has as a father, and you want him to talk to you and not another.

We must recognize that sons are influenced most times by their fathers, both natural and spiritual. Believe it or not, our sons learn about being a man primarily by watching their fathers. When I look at my life and how my father influenced me, I can say a lot of the things that I do, even down to the way that I dress, came from watching my father. It happens naturally. Whoever is before you the most is who you will model and look to for direction and guidance. As it was at home with my natural father, so it was in my spiritual life with my spiritual father, He is my blueprint of leadership. As I now lead, I look to him for direction and guidance. And can I say that most of the things that I have learned from my fathers were not done through sit down rounds, but instead they were caught through watching and being around them as they lived their lives before me. I want to challenge every father to spend time with your sons and be determined to make that connection with them.

As I reflect on my dad, a few of the things that he did to connect with his children was that he put up a basketball goal in the backyard, and we played basketball together. He would call us outside for a game, and he'd say things like, "come out here and let me school y'all real quick." Thinking about it now, it's still funny. He would get us up early on Saturday mornings to take us crabbing. We would drive to this place under a bridge near Ravenell, SC, and we would park the car, get all of our supplies and buckets and walk down this railroad track to several spots where we would set up to catch crabs. We would be out there for hours laughing and talking and seeing who would catch the biggest "blue". That's short for blue crab. I can see it now when he caught a big crab; he would hold it up in the net so we could all see it and say it like only he could, " Look at that BLUE!" And then when it was our turn, and we had a big one on the line, and we were pulling the line in slow, He would be behind us talking trash, "let me see what you are gonna do, dawg on it you bet not miss it." And if we missed it, He would just laugh at us and call us scrubs. My father is a funny guy, y'all. We would cut the yard together, wash the cars together, sit on the porch after cutting the grass that evening, and just listen to music and laugh and talk. There are just so many things that I think about as I write this, knowing now that this was his way of building a relationship with his children. When I think about my Spiritual father, Apostle Simmons, he is such a people's person. He's a father in his own right. As I reflected upon him in my early years of being under his ministry, he would invite us over to the house with his family for dinner, I felt just like one of his natural sons. I would play basketball in the driveway at his house with his sons and some of the other brothers from the church; we would lay down in the den while he sat in his lazy boy and watch tv, mainly the football games, laughing and talking. Over the years, I ended up at the big table in his house for marriage counseling, preparing to get married to Lady Baxter. We used to go out to eat together, ride the church bus while he or Uncle Moses drove us to his appointments to preach. There was so much that I learned and am continuing to learn from him about life, family, and ministry. A lot of these experiences that I have reflected upon, most of our sons now will know nothing about, because things in our world have changed so drastically. A lot of these things are not even done anymore. I thank God for the time in which he allowed me to come up in, naturally and spiritually. You just learn a lot by just being around a person. To be a father, you've got to be willing to let sons get close to you with respect as the standard and parameter. Close doesn't mean common. When we talk about becoming common with someone, we are speaking of becoming so familiar with them until you lose honor and respect for who they are in your life. There is danger in becoming familiar. You can't receive from someone you don't respect. An English writer by the name of Geoffrey Chaucer said, " familiarity breeds contempt." When we become too familiar with a Leader, before we know it, we cross lines that should not be crossed. We say things that we should not say, many times at the wrong time and in front of the wrong people, consequently resulting in shame, embarrassment, and disrespect to the Leader. Both biological and spiritual parents must draw a line or set a boundary to ensure that this doesn't happen to them. If you don't think your children won't shame you, let them do what they want to do in your home without you correcting them, and they'll show you something when they get out of that home in the public. Listen, if you don't train, correct, and discipline your children in your home, they will, at some point, embarrass and disrespect you in public. What you allow in private, will often be displayed in public, if not checked. So be cautious of sons becoming too familiar. Just a few things I've learned over the years of living and serving: We don't call our fathers by their first names, not because we don't know it, but to keep the proper level of respect for them. We don't talk back, argue, and become loud and boisterous towards our fathers. These are signs of disrespect. You don't ignore him or walk away from him when he's talking to you. You stand there respectfully and receive what he's saying, even if you disagree with what he is saying to you, and when the time allows, you respond respectfully. Never argue with your father in front of others. Talk with him privately, but never at any time disrespect him by shouting, responding sharply, or using bad language or having a bad spirit. To be allowed close and to be called a son is a privilege. Sons under no circumstances should ever disrespect their fathers. When someone takes the time to cultivate you, nurture you and build you, don't ever get beside yourself and become common and step out of your sonship to try to become equal with them. Settle yourself, check your spirit and then approach, if need be, respectfully.

As fathers and sons connect, there must be so much trust that communication is made easy. Develop such a bond with each other that all conversations can be held in confidence. Sons need to talk about more than just church and ministry. They have a life outside of church and ministry, just like you do. Sometimes we avoid the crucial conversations in the home and the church. When we avoid these conversations, we leave our sons to find their own way and develop their own mindset of how things should be done. Spiritual dads, as a part of your son's development, there need to be conversations held about life, family, education, work, financial stability, sex, and relationships. With the way of the world today, there is an ever-increasing presence of what seems to be fast money, sex, and different kinds of relationships on every platform. Sons need to understand that nothing falls in their laps out of the sky. You must work for everything you want. James 2:14-26 talks about the fact that *faith without works is dead*. We can say all day that we believe God for anything, but real faith makes steps towards the possession of it. Faith is an action word. It causes us to do something. Move! They need to know what the word says about it all. Your voice is critical in this process. Take the time to teach them and then be prepared for their questions. All of this is a part of that father and son connectivity.

Chapter 6

TOUGH LOVE

Hebrews 12:6-7 King James Version (KJV)

For whom the Lord loveth he chasteneth, and scourgeth every son whom he receiveth. If ye endure chastening, God dealeth with you as with sons; for what son is he whom the father chasteneth not?

Proverbs 3:11-12 King James Version (KJV)

My son, despise not the chastening of the Lord; neither be weary of his correction: For whom the Lord loveth he correcteth; even as a father the son in whom he delighteth.

Brothers and sisters, when we examine these two passages of scripture, we see the definition of "Tough Love" in full effect. We discover in these passages and others throughout the Bible that God is NOT AGAINST DISCIPLINE. As a matter of fact, not only is he for discipline, but his word tells us how to do it. *"Do everything with love."* (1 Corinthians 16:14) A father's correction is never to harm his son, but rather to help him and to keep him walking the right direction with the right mindset and spirit. Discipline, chastisement, correction, rebuke, and reproof are all necessary in our making process in order to ensure an example that people can follow and respect. Look at what Solomon says in these Proverbs concerning the necessity of discipline.

Prov.13:1 (BSB Translation)

A wise son heeds his father's discipline, but a mocker does not listen to rebuke.

Prov. 13:24 (BSB translation)

He who spares the rod hates his son, but he who loves him disciplines him diligently.

When you know your father's heart, then you know that when he has to apply discipline, it's only "Tough Love." When we define this expression, it means to be strict or stern with someone close to you in order to help them overcome a problem. They will ultimately benefit from your tough love in the long run. It is given to produce maturity or growth, responsibility, accountability, and stability. There is an expression that says, "To show somebody some tough love today will save them heartache in the future." You may not understand why your father seems so " hard" right now, but endure the hardness, because it will be for your benefit in the future. He sees your potential. He wants to produce a stable son. These scriptures make it very clear to us that a father that doesn't show his son tough love doesn't love him at all. When you are allowed to do what you want to do, how you want to do it, and when you want to do it, without any accountability or taking any responsibility for your actions, you are not being raised or properly handled to become someone respectable. With this kind of freedom as a son, you will most likely have no respect for authority and will walk around in pride. If we're going to get anywhere in God, we must have a spirit of humility. The truth of the matter is Tough Love hurts; however, it is a tool that has been given to bring forth humility in us. As much as we say, "correct me when I'm wrong," "pull my coat tail if I go too far or if I am out of order", most don't mean it. The proof will be in the test. When it is done to you, it won't feel good, and guess what, you will feel that thing. The embarrassment, that shameful attitude that comes on you will often bring you to tears and your heart to feel crushed. If you don't keep in the front of your mind that this is my father and he loves me, and this has been done for my making, your flesh will have you in a place where you'll be ready to walk away from what you need in your life the most. Someone who loves you enough will not let you walk around thinking you're right when you're in error.

I want you to evolve into a son that understands that when you are corrected, disciplined, or rebuked by your father that it's him keeping you from yourself. Self is selfish, prideful, and it feels that it's always right and will do all it can do to justify its actions, no matter what it is that it has done. We have to be protected from our own selves. This is one of the purposes of that Spiritual Father in our lives. Someone that would be close enough to know us and correct us in order to save us from ourselves. You need someone in your life that you trust that can say to you, "You are about to damage yourself, so let me help you." Real love doesn't let you stay in error without letting you know that you're in error. I have to say it like that because we're living in a time now where people know that they are in error and will try to justify it with their own interpretation of scripture. They form their own opinions or even excuses, instead of submitting to authority and the truth of God's word. This is what the scriptures tell us to do:

Philippians 2:3-4 New Living Translation (NLT)

Don't be selfish; don't try to impress others. Be humble, thinking of others as better than yourselves. Don't look out only for your own interests, but take an interest in others, too.

1 Peter 5:6 King James Version (KJV)

Humble yourselves therefore under the mighty hand of God, that he may exalt you in due time:

Learn to endure tough love. Continue to serve. Continue to be faithful. Continue to love your father. Learn how to take it and keep it moving. I challenge you to change your mindset about your father's chastisement and receive the truth of God's word concerning it. He's taking the time to sharpen you. He sees something in you that can be of benefit to the Kingdom. Don't throw your greatness away by allowing pride to push you out of your place of receiving from him. Don't just be receptive to the praise that he gives you, but also be receptive to the correction that will come as needed. We are going to make mistakes in our process of evolution. It's bound to happen because we are not perfect people. When it does happen, and you're corrected, receive it, adjust, and advance. KEEP GOING!! You will thank him later for his tough love. John 3:16 says, *"For God so loved the world, that he gave his ONLY begotten SON, that whosoever believeth in him should not perish, but have everlasting life."* I've read this passage and have preached this passage many times, but it wasn't until writing this particular segment in this book that I thought about the fact that the decision that God made to allow his one and only son to come into this sinful world to die for the sins of it was a tough move that he had to make, but it was for the bigger picture. It was a win-win situation. Jesus would die and be resurrected and be given the name that would be above every name. His life would be given for the souls of many that would believe in His name would be able to be reconciled back to God, the Father. Sons, if you would just submit to the process, you could be the very one to save something of your father's from its demise. What he created doesn't have to die; it can live through you. Jesus shows us that sons will have to sacrifice oftentimes for the other souls that the father has to reach. One thing we know about Jesus is that He was willing to do whatever it took to please the Father. Thank God for the Son. (Hebrews 10:4-12)

MAN UP

As I think about how Jesus handled those that walked closest to him, Jesus was kind and caring toward them, but then he didn't hold any punches either when it came to that inner circle. One of those moments that stick out the most to me is found in the Gospel, according to Matthew 16:21-28.

Matthew 16:21-28 New Living Translation (NLT)

Jesus Predicts His Death

From then on Jesus[a] began to tell his disciples plainly that it was necessary for him to go to Jerusalem, and that he would suffer many terrible things at the hands of the elders, the leading priests, and the teachers of religious law. He would be killed, but on the third day he would be raised from the dead.

But Peter took him aside and began to reprimand him[b] for saying such things. "Heaven forbid, Lord," he said. "This will never happen to you!" Jesus turned to Peter and said, "Get away from me, Satan! You are a dangerous trap to me. You are seeing things merely from a human point of view, not from God's."

Then Jesus said to his disciples, "If any of you wants to be my follower, you must give up your own way, take up your cross, and follow me. If you try to hang on to your life, you will lose it. But if you give up your life for my sake, you will save it. And what do you benefit if you gain the whole world but lose your own soul?[c] Is anything worth more than your soul? For the Son of Man will come with his angels in the glory of his father and will judge all people according to their deeds. And I tell you the truth, some standing here right now will not die before they see the Son of Man coming in his Kingdom."

In this text, Jesus was on his way to fulfill his ultimate purpose. He was giving His inner circle the inside scoop of what was going to happen so that they would be prepared for it. Peter, who without a shadow of a doubt, loves Jesus, one who was strongly attached to him, could not bear to think of Jesus being put to death. He moves or responds out of his heart for Jesus, many commentaries say that he grabs Jesus's hand as a friend and says to him, " Heaven forbid, Lord, This will never happen." In other words, "not if I can help it!" The scriptures use the words rebuked or reprimanded, but when we interpret and understand the respect and honor that these men had for Jesus, we discover that these words meant that he was admonishing him. Peter was not trying to assume authority over Jesus, but he earnestly expressed his feelings that he did not want this to take place. He wanted to protect Jesus. This is the same spirit that Jesus had to deal with in the garden of Gethsemane, which caused Peter to draw the sword on His behalf (John 18:10). Peter was overstepping his bounds. He should have simply been submissive and not have interfered. As sons, you've got to know your boundaries. Know when to speak and when not to speak. Know when to stand up, and then, know when to get out of the way. This was purpose being fulfilled, and there was nothing that Peter could do to stop it from coming to pass. Jesus's response to Peter was very stern and sharp. Jesus turned to Peter and said, "Get behind me, Satan," or also translated, " Get away from me, Satan." You are a dangerous trap to me. You are seeing things from a human point of view and not from God's. According to Elliot's Commentary for English Readers, Jesus's response to Peter was as hard as it was, because it took him back to what he went through in the wilderness with Satan, the Tempter, himself. In other words, you telling me that I shouldn't have to go through this is like telling me that I can get something for nothing. This was a renewal of the temptation. As in to suggest that He could receive a crown without a cross. Jesus could not draw back from the path that His Father had aligned for Him. He had to go through this way. It was divinely orchestrated. He continued aloud so that the others could hear him. Many times the group will push up the one that doesn't mind talking to speak for everyone, so Jesus wanted all of them to hear this rebuke. He says, "you are a dangerous trap to me." Meaning you are a stumbling block, an impediment, or a hindrance to me. Peter's feelings were getting in the way and, thus, ultimately trying to stop Jesus's future. See, Peter wasn't considering the whole prophecy, just the first part. If he had taken time to dissect the rest of what Jesus said, maybe he would have kept quiet. Jesus said as I paraphrase, they will kill me, but in three days, I'm going to rise again. Therefore, what is taking place here is that Peter is hindering and not helping his Master's work. Jesus knew without a doubt that Peter loved him, but Peter needed to get out of the way of the will of God for Jesus's life. What I love about this text is that after the rebuke, the story doesn't record that Peter left Jesus. It doesn't say that Peter was angry with Jesus, nor does it say that Peter exchanged any more words with Jesus concerning this. Peter took it! One thing we know about Peter is that he wasn't soft. He had tough skin. I've discovered over my years of serving that you cannot wear your feelings on your shoulders. When you are a student, you have to learn how to take what we call constructive criticism. An assessment that will help make you better. We didn't always get all of the answers right, but thank God that the teacher didn't just check it right but marked it wrong and then came back and showed me how to get it right the next time. **Stop letting folks pass with the wrong answers!** Sometimes we are wrong and have to be checked so that we don't continue to think that we are right. In your time of prayer and meditation, ask God to toughen you up so that you won't take correction or chastisement personally. True fathers are not out to hurt you but to help you. Listen, you're going to be taking over the reign one day, and they need to know that you're strong enough to carry it on! No more sensitive sons, but strong sons. **Man Up**! You can handle it, that's why God strategically planted you where he did and under the tutelage of who he did. It was in my last year of High School, and I struggled in math horribly. I knew I needed this class in order to graduate, and I was trying all I could to do the work and pass my tests, but when I tell you that I struggled. I was a preacher during that time, but my teacher didn't care anything about that, she called me Mr. Baxter. She wanted that work done right. She knew that I was trying hard, so one day, she called me to the side as we were all exiting the classroom. She said,

"Mr. Baxter, come here and let me talk with you." She said to me, you've got to pass my class because I want you to graduate." She began to set up times for me to come and receive extra help and to work on my tests, and I did other work to get extra credit. That lady worked with me, and I passed her class and was able to graduate! She was so happy for me she came to the graduation cookout at my house that afternoon after graduation! I will never forget her as long as I live because she took the time to help me. She didn't give me a free pass, but she worked with me. If my answer was wrong, she let me know and then helped me to work that problem until I got it right. She could have failed me, but she decided to help me, and for that, I am eternally grateful. The moral of that story is in life, you don't graduate, by getting by, you graduate by doing the work! Sonship is work. Don't just sit under your father, but serve with him. Help him! Put your hands to the plow and don't look back (Luke 9:62). I saw something else in the text there in Matthew as it pertains to the continuance of Peter and Jesus's close relationship. That is, if we follow the story on over to the 17th chapter, verses 1 and 2, Peter still stayed close to Jesus, and his name is the first name called out of the other two that witnessed Jesus's transfiguration. Peter was privileged to witness what many of the other disciples did not get to witness.

Matthew 17:1-2 New Living Translation (NLT)

The Transfiguration

Six days later Jesus took Peter and the two brothers, James and John, and led them up a high mountain to be alone. As the men watched, Jesus' appearance was transformed so that his face shone like the sun, and his clothes became as white as light.

Those that will allow themselves to experience the process of evolution will ultimately experience the power of elevation. Through it all STAY SUBMITTED.

ABOUT THE AUTHOR
BISHOP DAVID L. BAXTER, JR.
Senior Pastor, Greater True Light Ministries Sounds of Praise
Founder & Senior Pastor, The Cathedral of Hope Sounds of Praise

Bishop David L. Baxter, Jr. is the son of David and (the late) Bonnie Baxter of Summerville, SC. He graduated from Summerville High School and attended Claflin College.

Bishop Baxter was saved at an early age and recognized that God had His hands upon him. He attended Shiloh FBH Church under the leadership of Elder Patrick Frazier, Sr., and it was at Shiloh FBH Church he grew and sought the Lord. Dedicated to the call of service, he attended Sunday School, sang on the choir, ushered, and was a member of the YPI and other auxiliaries in the church. At the age of 16, Bishop Baxter was called into the ministry.

Following the lead of God, Bishop Baxter then joined Emanuel Baptist Church, where Pastor Robert A. Vandross was pastor. Here he continued his growth in ministry. In revival after revival, he preached under the anointing and unction of the Holy Ghost.

Once his season at Emanuel Baptist Church ended, God moved him to Greater New Bethel Sounds of Praise under the dynamic and charismatic leadership of Apostle Allen H. Simmons. At Greater New Bethel, Bishop Baxter's ministerial duties expanded. He served as an associate minister, Bible Study instructor, while continuing to minister in revivals.

On April 30, 2003, he was appointed Pastor of Deliverance Cathedral Sounds of Praise in Columbia, SC, where he served for seven years preaching and teaching deliverance and restoration. During this time, God directed him to birth another ministry, The Cathedral of Hope Sounds of Praise in Reevesville, SC. January 1, 2006, began the first of many anointed services, where he preached, taught, and brought hope to those he reached.

On October 23, 2010, he became the Senior Pastor of Greater True Light Ministries in Myrtle Beach, SC. The Most Reverend, Chief Apostle Allen H. Simmons consecrated him into the Bishopric on May 16, 2015 during the Seventh Triennial of the Sounds of Praise Pentecostal Fellowship Ministries, Inc. He currently serves as the Sounds of Praise Columba District Bishop (The Judah District) and National Bishop of Evangelism.

Bishop Baxter has been married to Lady Kenyetta McMillian Baxter for 19 years, who serves faithfully with him in ministry. She is without question his #1

Supporter. To their union, God blessed them with three beautiful children: Shekinah', and twins, Kyle and Kyah'.

Bishop Baxter is a man after God's own heart. He lives what he preaches and is a man of honor and integrity. He serves the Body of Christ with his trust and faith in God, his teaching, his preaching, his compassion, his humility, and most of all, his love of and for God's people. He is truly "A Man of God."

www.ingramcontent.com/pod-product-compliance
Lightning Source LLC
Chambersburg PA
CBHW070939160426
43193CB00011B/1745